TWO FOR THE ROAD

A RELATIONSHIP MANUAL DESIGNED FOR HIM... *AND ESSENTIAL FOR HER*

Gale D. Stanton, MA, OTR/L

Cover design by Kim Greyer.

Printed and published in the United States of America

TREATY OAK PUBLISHERS

ISBN-10: 1-943658-02-1
ISBN-13: 978-1-943658-02-2

_____

Life is a highway

I want to ride it all night long

If you're going my way

I want to drive it all night long

Tom Cochrane

This book is dedicated to all of the optimistic individuals in the world who fall in love seeking a long-term, committed relationship. It is for those of us who would never board a plane knowing that it had a 50/50 chance of crashing, yet we enter into marriage with that same awareness. Two for the Road is dedicated to lovers, dreamers, and doers, and to the Motor City. It is there where I fell in love with the automobile and thrill of the road trip. Life is all about the journey and those we choose to ride with along the way.

GALE D. STANTON has studied and worked in mental health and wellness for over twenty years. She holds a Master of Arts degree in Counseling from Oakland University, Rochester Hills, Michigan, and has worked as a Registered Occupational Therapist in psychiatric hospitals in Michigan and Florida. She became a Pediatric Therapy Specialist for California Children Services prior to becoming a Program Director for a private college in San Diego, California, where she taught classes in Life-Span Development and Psychosocial Functioning. As an educator and program director, she developed an Occupational Therapy Assistant program accredited by the Accreditation Council of Occupational Therapy Education.

Ms. Stanton has both personal and professional experience with marriage and divorce. Urged by female clients and associates to create a relationship book that men would actually read, she developed Two for the Road. Written in a manual format that appeals to men, the relationship principles in the book are universal to both sexes. She designed this unique relationship guide to get the conversation started between couples. Two for the Road includes content and interactive exercises that promote constructive dialogues instead of one-sided monologues.

Raised in the suburb Bloomfield Hills, Michigan, outside of Detroit (the "Motor City"), she currently resides in a suburb of Dallas, Texas. As a trained therapist and educator, she has several other relationship books underway that span the life stages of intimate relationships.

CONTENTS

CONTENTS

It is advised that individuals should read this manual from beginning to end when considering being involved in a committed relationship. Designed in the format of a car manual, it is a practical resource guide aimed at helping couples navigate the bumpy road of romance. Two for the Road is a legitimate tool developed to assist both men and women in driving their relationship to obtain the maximum benefit and pleasure from it. This clever self-help aid simplifies relationship dynamics into basic, concrete and easy-to-understand terms. It is a "how to" book about relationship survival and is a must for understanding, maintaining, and restoring the sometimes difficult ride associated with love and marriage. Who you decide to travel through life with and how you get there are major fundamentals of the book. Two for the Road establishes that great relationships are created. They do not happen by accident.

INDEX

A good place to quickly locate information about the relationship is in the Index located in the back of this manual. It is an alphabetical list of what is in this manual and the page number where it can be found.

⚠ **WARNING**

This symbol means there is something that could hurt you or other people.

🚫 This symbol means "DO NOT do this... or DO NOT let this happen."

SAFETY WARNINGS AND SYMBOLS

There are a number of safety cautions or warnings in this book.

A box with the word **WARNING** is used to tell about things that could hurt you or the relationship if you were to ignore the warning. Often the warning is a fact that should be considered in relationships and other times the warning is a hazard that needs to be avoided.

A circle with a slash through it means "DO NOT do this… or DO NOT let this happen."

INTERACTIVE EXERCISES

There are a number of exercises included in this book intended to promote discovery and understanding between partners.

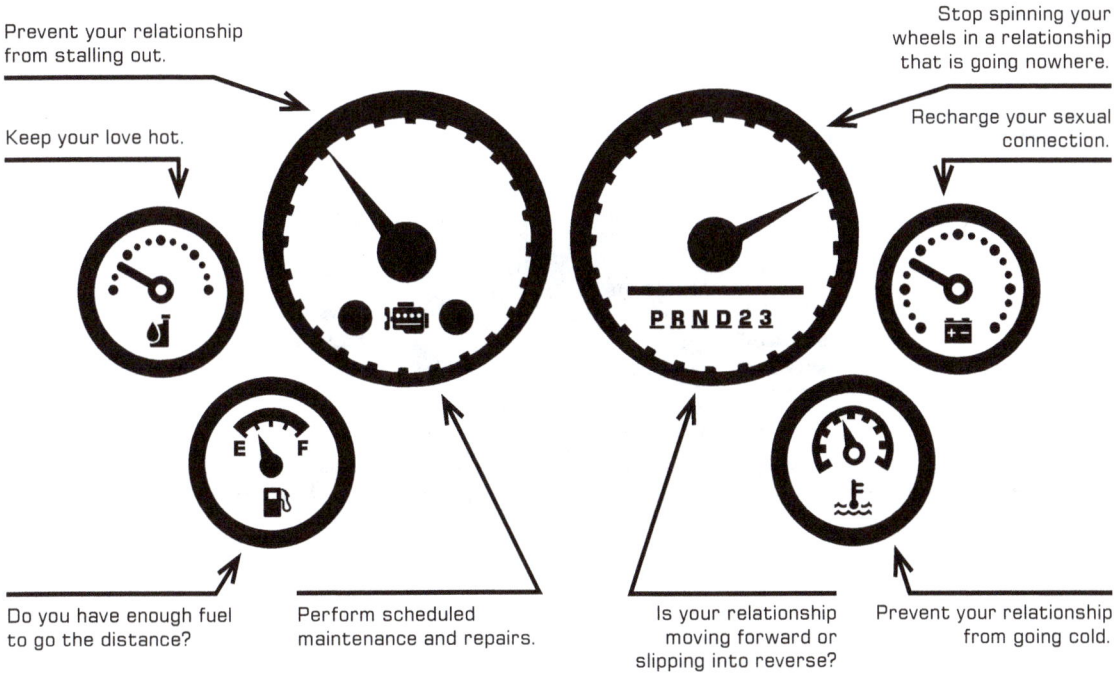

Prevent your relationship from stalling out.

Keep your love hot.

Stop spinning your wheels in a relationship that is going nowhere.

Recharge your sexual connection.

Do you have enough fuel to go the distance?

Perform scheduled maintenance and repairs.

Is your relationship moving forward or slipping into reverse?

Prevent your relationship from going cold.

How to communicate effectively in your relationship.

How to determine where your relationship is headed.

02:14

How to make your relationship fun and exciting.

How to control the temperature of the relationship...hot or cold. It's up to you.

TEST DRIVE
(DATING)

TYPE OF VEHICLE – How would you categorize your partner? A luxury sedan, economical smart car, and tough performing pick-up truck are very dissimilar vehicles. They serve different functions that address the unique needs of their owners. Appreciate what they do well and don't expect them to be everything to everybody. Pamela Anderson and Barbara Walters do not perform the same function. One is famous for her bombshell sex appeal, both on screen and off. The other is a well-known and accomplished journalist who has interviewed world leaders. Both could be categorized as television personalities and may have similar roles off-screen such as working mothers, still they are vastly different individuals. Each understands their notorious positions in life and neither attempts the other's profession. Know what type of partner best suits you before entering into a relationship for a more desirable outcome.

TEST DRIVE THE VEHICLE – Is it a suitable for you? Do you enjoy the ride?

⚠ **WARNING:** The look of relationships and marriage today is very different from 100 years ago. Henry Ford originally produced the Model T in one prototype and color only. Today, vehicles consist of numerous models, styles and colors. The same is true about the roles and opportunities that exist for both men and women. The options are endless and should be considered for the most appropriate fit to ensure a more harmonious relationship.

⚠ **WARNING:** Break your relationship in slowly even though it is tempting to go fast amidst all the excitement during the infatuation stage. Speed kills. Don't jump into the commitment phase too fast or you may experience buyer's remorse later on.

THE PUSH START BUTTON – What turns your partner on and what turns them off? Not only in bed, but in life. Pay attention to their take on the human condition. How do they react to kissing in public or bad manners at the dinner table? What about gum or tobacco chewing? Discover their pet peeves as well as their passions.

What are the major "hot buttons" for your partner? Good and bad. Do they love concerts but hate sports? What are their interests and how do they feel about yours? Are they more of an environmentalist or an industrialist? Conservative or a liberal? Where do they want to go in love and in life?

> ⚠ **WARNING:** Don't rally and pretend to be someone you are not. Going to the Opera may make you appear more cultured as well as please your partner; however, it will be futile if you hate it. Be honest about who you are, otherwise it will only confuse and complicate things later on.

THE CRUISE CONTROL FEATURE – Though convenient for long distance driving, it is tempting but can be dangerous if used for extended periods of time. It allows you to zone out while in the driver's seat. Remain alert to what is going on around you. A common mistake is for one partner to assume that all is going well in the relationship only to be blindsided when the other one wants out. Never assume that your partner feels the same way about the relationship as you do. Just because you are happy doesn't mean your partner shares your joy. Pay attention to the signs and signals that your mate sends you along the way.

> ⚠ **WARNING:** Always pay close attention to the changing road conditions, especially when using the cruise control feature.

THE VOICE COMMAND FEATURE – Instructions are included for this feature to function properly. Contrary to popular opinion, couples do communicate with each other. However, most do not know how to do it effectively. When you are speaking consider the following:

- It requires quiet in the vehicle. (Converse with no distractions.)
- Do not speak until the listening light appears. (Make certain your partner is listening and not tuning you out.)
- Speak naturally without long pauses. (Gather you thoughts before articulating them. Be deliberate and choose your words wisely.)
- Do not yell or raise your voice.
- Do not interrupt or you will have to start over.

WHAT SPARKS MOST OF THE CONFLICTS BETWEEN YOU TWO? – Are they about money, insensitivity, excessive drinking of alcohol or the children? Are these disagreements handled by temper tantrums or the silent treatment? Do you have constructive conversations that bring you closer together or destructive altercations that chip away at the foundation of your relationship?

IS YOUR PARTNER TOO PREOCCUPIED WITH LOOKING IN THE REARVIEW MIRROR? – Are they more absorbed in their past and what could have, would have, or should have been? Or are they positive and proactive seeking what lies ahead down the road beyond the windshield? Did they learn from their mistakes or do they use them as an excuse for repeated failures? Is their glass half-empty or half-full? Do they see problems as challenges or insurmountable hurdles?

IS YOUR RELATIONSHIP DEFINED AS MORE HIGH PERFORMANCE OR LOW MAINTENANCE? – There are advantages and liabilities associated with both. High performance, though more flashy and exciting, involves drama. Low maintenance is less thrilling but more practical, both emotionally and economically. In other words, don't complain when someone spends time and money on themselves for hair, manicures, pedicures, make-up and clothes if their keen sense of style is what attracted you to them in the first place. It comes with the territory.

WHO IS IN THE DRIVER'S SEAT? – Don't assume that gender has anything to do with who is in control. Typically one person is more dominant in driving the relationship. However, important decision making may shift depending on the circumstances and may be role specific. One partner may be the bread winner while the other is a stay-at-home parent. Defining who makes the calls in what areas can prevent the two of you from constantly butting heads.

> **WARNING:** ASK THESE SAME QUESTIONS OF YOURSELF. Know your own features and controls first before confronting your partner. Self-awareness is the first step in assessing if someone is a good fit for you. Self-disclosure is the next step. Equally as important as you discovering how your partner works is disclosing to them exactly how you work. If you are the jealous and possessive type, this will become apparent over time. Your partner may be flattered by your determination to keep them all to yourself, or they may feel suffocated and annoyed by it. Be straightforward about who you are and what it is that you expect from a relationship.

STEERING WHEEL – It is imperative that you steer your relationship with every turn. Be deliberate about staying on the road even if you get lost. Keep two hands on the wheel and don't permit your relationship to drift off course. Careless driving may result in a simple warning or a potentially fatal crash. Expecting that your relationship will automatically progress in the right direction is dangerous.

TIRE PRESSURE MONITORING SYSTEM – It is necessary to recognize the internal and external pressures affecting your wellbeing as well as your relationship. Failure to maintain proper tire pressure could result in tire failure, blowouts, loss of control, vehicle rollover, and personal injury. Deflating tires (egos) occur with daily wear and tear. Periodically inflating tires, like egos, are necessary to keep things running smoothly.

ENGINE COOLANT TEMPERATURE – This illuminates when the temperature of the coolant is too high. Stop the vehicle immediately and let the engine cool. When you and your partner are engaged in an overly heated argument or discussion, shut the system down completely. Do not continue to drive the vehicle as it could result in a complete engine meltdown. Walk away and wait for things to cool before starting it up again.

THE HISTORY OF YOUR VEHICLE

Understanding the past history and reputation of the vehicle along with the service and maintenance record can help to predict its future performance. Whether someone was raised around country clubs or camp grounds, they will most likely have a preference for them later in life. If someone grew up on the ocean, it will be a challenge to get them to live in the desert. Most importantly, if your partner came from an abusive or unloving environment, this will definitely affect how they view and deal with the world. Know what kind of background they came from and what life events have shaped them as a child.

⚠️ **WARNING:** If your partner has been in a major crash and totaled, make sure that you know what parts have been damaged and that the necessary repairs have been made. Life experience can have both positive and negative effects on people, thus the relationship. We all bring our baggage with us. It is imperative to know what's in the trunk.

FOUR POINT INSPECTION

HISTORY

DATE	ODOMETER	SERVICE

What is the make-up of their family history?
A Chevrolet can be a $12,000 Spark or a $112,000 Corvette. Both are in significantly different classes regarding performance, quality, and cost. Socioeconomic backgrounds, childhood experiences, values, educational and religious upbringing all affect relationships and need to be addressed. If you are Jewish and your partner is a Christian, the Christmas tree is likely to be an issue. If one person has a formal education and the other doesn't, improper grammar may incite a dispute.

MECHANICS	**Look under the hood.** Inspect the chassis to see if it is bent. A nice paint job can make the vehicle look good but cannot govern how well it runs. The guts are vitally important. Biology is destiny. Differences in the brain and overall anatomy of men and women create different realities. Recognize the inner workings (mechanics) to better understand the person.
REGION	**What part of the country is the vehicle from originally?** Regions of the country have certain reputations for a reason. An SUV from Texas may not come equipped with heated seats. A convertible is not practical to drive in Arizona during the summer months. In other words, a Southerner may find New Yorkers rude, and California beaches are most certainly not the Jersey Shore. Understand, respect, and appreciate the differences where each of you were raised.
MILEAGE	**How many miles are on the vehicle?** More important than the year the car was built is the mileage on the odometer. Is your partner worldly or sheltered? Have they been to Europe or even out of their own state? The mileage also addresses the developmental life stage of your partner. Someone in their 30's may be retired and golfing daily while someone in their 50's may want to have a baby or start a new career. Don't judge someone simply by their chronological age.

If your vehicle ever needs a new odometer installed, the new one will be set to the correct mileage total of the old odometer. **Do not conceal or attempt to alter your life stage for someone else.**

HANDLING PROCEDURES

QUESTIONS

A. Does the vehicle handle better when driven fast or slow? High energy people require a lot of activity to prevent them from getting restless or bored. Lower energy people prefer moving at a slower pace that may include additional quiet time. If they are an extrovert, they get energy from being in the company of others and enjoy bouncing ideas off of them. However, introverts prefer processing information internally and are more reserved in public. Fast or slow?

YOUR ANSWERS

_____

_____

_____

_____

_____

_____

_____

QUESTIONS   **YOUR ANSWERS**

B. When all systems are operating at full capacity,
how often does the battery need recharging?
Power naps, cat naps, and a full night sleep may
be required for positive outcomes in mood,
energy and general wellbeing. Are yours in sync
with your partners? Are you an early riser while
they are a night owl? Does this create problems
with your daily schedules?

C. How does your vehicle handle in bad weather?   **YOUR ANSWERS**
The ride is always smooth when things are going
well, but what happens when confronted with
adverse conditions? Does the vehicle slide all
over the road and wind up in a ditch or does it
remain on the path destination bound? Does
it get stuck frequently requiring assistance or
can it switch into four-wheel-drive to get out of
rough spots?

D. Does the vehicle handle better off-roading in   **YOUR ANSWERS**
the dirt or traveling on major freeways? Does
it excel in the city or the country? Do your
preferences match your partner's in a way that
can assure greater compatibility?

HANDLING PROCEDURES

QUESTIONS

E. What are the average miles-per-gallon for a tank of gas? How often does it need refueling? Are you willing to spend the time and money to keep the engine running? People, similar to autos, require varying frequencies for replenishing. Someone may necessitate constant encouragement while another may only need it once in a while.

YOUR ANSWERS

_____

_____

_____

_____

_____

F. Drive it around family and friends to get their take on it. What comments do they share with you? Those that know you best can help you to determine if it is or isn't a good fit for you and why. Though the ultimate decision is yours alone to make, others can provide additional information that may prove useful.

YOUR ANSWERS

_____

_____

_____

_____

_____

WARNING: The problem with the opinion of family and friends is that they may not always be forthcoming or honest about their feelings so as not to hurt you. Also, if they do give their feedback, it may be coming from another place. Such as, misery loves company, or jealousy, or other self-motivated responses. Take it with a grain of salt. Your gut will ultimately help you to determine the right thing to do.

BOTTOM LINE – Can you afford what you are buying? Are the emotional and financial demands associated with the relationship too great? Are you willing to do what is necessary to keep the relationship machine running properly?

For instance, you may be in love with someone who sets the bar higher than you ever anticipated. Say that your partner wants to have six children, all attending private schools, and live in Beverly Hills, California. Knowing that they will be disappointed if they don't get those things and realizing that you cannot provide them creates a no win situation, one in which both of you will potentially end up being miserable.

What happens if you fall in love with a person from a foreign country who refuses to leave their homeland? Are you prepared to move a continent away and leave your family and friends? Are you able to deal with the cultural differences and adapt to their customs, forsaking your own? You need to factor in the cost of the relationship to your general wellbeing. What price must you pay to preserve the partnership? Is it worth it?

WARNING: If you can't afford it, don't buy it! Simply because you love it doesn't mean that it is right for you. Consider all of the variables regarding the test drive, the purchase, and the ongoing maintenance to make a well-informed decision.

CASH FOR CARS

It has been reported that money is the number one reason why couples battle. As individuals, we all have our own unique relationship with money. Rarely do couples share the same history, spending habits, and income levels. Each brings a different reality regarding money into the relationship.

Answer the following questions TRUE or FALSE and discuss the details with your partner.

As a child, I was given the things that I asked for without having to do chores to acquire them.

O TRUE   O FALSE

My mother and father both contributed to the family income.

O TRUE   O FALSE

I had my own savings account before the age of twelve.

O TRUE   O FALSE

I observed my family struggling financially.

O TRUE   O FALSE

My family dined out at restaurants at least three times a week.

O TRUE   O FALSE

I earned money as a child, before the age of twelve (not from family). If true, what did you do?

O TRUE   O FALSE

My first part time job was during high school. If true, what did you do?

O TRUE   O FALSE

My parents bought my first car.
○ TRUE   ○ FALSE

My first fulltime job was before the age of twenty-one. If true, what did you do?
○ TRUE   ○ FALSE

My parents paid for my college education.
○ TRUE   ○ FALSE

I have taken out a loan and paid it back.
○ TRUE   ○ FALSE

I have defaulted on a loan or a credit card.
○ TRUE   ○ FALSE

Credit cards should only be used in emergencies.
○ TRUE   ○ FALSE

Discussing a budget is uncomfortable but living on one is essential.
○ TRUE   ○ FALSE

The man should pay for the date.
○ TRUE   ○ FALSE

The man should pay for the majority of the household expenses.
○ TRUE   ○ FALSE

I prefer to possess a few designer items rather than a closet full of bargains.
○ TRUE   ○ FALSE

I prefer to lease a car as opposed to own one.
○ TRUE   ○ FALSE

Owning a home is better than renting one.

○ TRUE   ○ FALSE

A fifteen-year mortgage is better than a thirty-year mortgage.

○ TRUE   ○ FALSE

Gambling is recreational and harmless.

○ TRUE   ○ FALSE

A financial advisor is a must.

○ TRUE   ○ FALSE

Ten percent of your salary should be put in savings each year.

○ TRUE   ○ FALSE

You will need close to a million dollars in savings to retire comfortably.

○ TRUE   ○ FALSE

Living for today means that you cannot save for tomorrow.

○ TRUE   ○ FALSE

Relocation for a better job is preferable even if you must leave family and friends.

○ TRUE   ○ FALSE

New is better than used.

○ TRUE   ○ FALSE

A fund set up for charitable contributions is a must.

○ TRUE   ○ FALSE

Quality healthcare is nonnegotiable.

○ TRUE   ○ FALSE

I plan to work until I have children.

O TRUE   O FALSE

I plan to retire at the age of 65.

O TRUE   O FALSE

Bankruptcy is always an option.

O TRUE   O FALSE

If I run out of money a family member will support me.

O TRUE   O FALSE

I believe productivity and the old fashioned work ethic make people more attractive.

O TRUE   O FALSE

Real estate is always a good investment.

O TRUE   O FALSE

I earn more so I am entitled to spend more.

O TRUE   O FALSE

I am the breadwinner so I get to tell you what to do and what to spend.

O TRUE   O FALSE

The mother should receive child support even when parents split custody.

O TRUE   O FALSE

Alimony is fair.

O TRUE   O FALSE

It's okay to loan a substantial amount of money to a friend if they need it.

O TRUE   O FALSE

I don't need a 401K because I am getting an inheritance from my parents.

○ TRUE   ○ FALSE

Owning a small business is better than working for a big one.

○ TRUE   ○ FALSE

Money is the root of all evil.

○ TRUE   ○ FALSE

Cash is king.

○ TRUE   ○ FALSE

A formal education is necessary in order to make a good living.

○ TRUE   ○ FALSE

Personal freedom is more important than a paycheck.

○ TRUE   ○ FALSE

1. Adams, Samuel, and Ben Young. **"The One: A Realistic Guide to Choosing Your Soul Mate."** Thomas Nelson, 2008.

2. Anderson, Lisa. **"The Dating Manifesto: A Drama-Free Plan For Pursuing Marriage With Purpose."** David C. Cook, 2015.

3. Ansari, Aziz and Eric Klinenberg. **"Modern Romance."** Penguin Press, 2015.

4. Argov, Sherry. **"Why Men Love Bitches: From Doormat to Dreamgirl – A Woman's Guide to Holding Her Own in a Relationship."** Adams Media, 2002.

5. Behrendt, Greg, and Liz Tuccillo. **"He's Just Not That Into You: The No Excuses Truth to Understanding Guys."** Gallery Books, 2009.

6. Browne, Joy. **"Dating for Dummies. For Dummies."** 2011.

7. Cloud, Henry, and John Townsend. **"Boundaries in Dating: How Healthy Choices Grow Healthy Relationships."** Zondervan, 2000.

8. Gray, John. **"Mars and Venus on a Date: A Guide for Navigating the 5 Stages of Dating to Create a Loving and Lasting Relationship."** Harper Perennial, 2005.

9. Stanley, Andy. **"The New Rules For Love, Sex and Dating."** Zondervan, 2015.

10. Warren, Neil Clark. **"Date... or Soul Mate? How to Know if Someone is Worth Pursuing in Two Dates or Less."** Thomas Nelson, 2005.

PURCHASING YOUR VEHICLE (MARRIAGE)

ANTICIPATE TROUBLE BEFORE IT STARTS BY KNOWING WHAT TO EXPECT – The journey is long and it is unrealistic to believe that there won't be challenges along the way. Be prepared for minor inconveniences and setbacks such as roadblocks and detours. Small emergencies that consist of minor traffic violations or collisions can be frustrating as well as costly.

NEW CAR SMELL – It goes away. In relationships this equates to about eighteen months to two years. That is when social scientists have determined that the infatuation stage ends and the real relationship begins. Knowing that this is a universal phenomenon can make the transition smoother and less disappointing for all.

FOCUS ON THE GOOD THINGS AND COUNT YOUR BLESSINGS – Maintain a positive outlook and remember why you fell in love with this person in the first place. Though the automatic adrenaline rush dissipates from when you first met, it can be recreated from time to time with some effort. The chrome still shines beneath

WARNING: This is when you begin to notice that many of those things that you loved about the other person initially are now driving you crazy. You thought your partner was so funny when you were first dating but now their jokes have become repetitive and annoying.

Sex every morning in the shower was amazing but now it just makes you late for work. That all-encompassing, butterfly-in-the-stomach obsession with your partner must subside in order for the two of you to go on with the business of living. It has to diminish some or no one would ever get anything done. When this happens… DON'T PANIC.

the dirt, it just needs to be dusted and polished occasionally. The hot and heavy infatuation portion of your relationship will fade much like the new car smell. However, great friendships rarely dwindle and actually intensify over the years. Being best friends can last forever and stand the test of time.

> ⚠ **WARNING:** Some people use children as insurance to stay married. This is a really bad idea. It is an antiquated concept, like having multiple children to toil on the family farm. It doesn't work in modern society.

THE WARRANTY – It expires. Designed for peace of mind, it's easy to guarantee that a vehicle will perform with few problems when it is new and requires little upkeep. When you make those vows to be together forever and never part, you mean them at the time. People generally don't go into marriage anticipating a divorce. However, as time passes, it requires more energy and determination to deal with unexpected difficulties and forks in the road. Ongoing maintenance and repairs take their toll. What once felt so effortless and natural now requires a conscientious resolve to stay together.

INSURANCE – Most people don't have insurance for their marriage, although some do have prenuptial agreements. That said, the best insurance for any marriage is to keep it happy and secure. Refer to the section on security features in a relationship: communication, love and respect, humor, intimacy and sex, along with recreation and fun. Prioritizing these things and working on them daily insures that you will have a better chance surviving a relationship long term.

SCRATCHES AND DENTS – Expect them. There are certain things over which you have no control. No matter how you try and safeguard the beauty of your shiny new vehicle, bad things are going to happen to take the luster away. Disagreements, arguments, misunderstandings, and unexpected troubles will arise. Know that they can be repaired and restored.

DATE FOREVER

- Flirt, flirt and flirt.

- Kiss – make out.

- Be spontaneous and mix it up. Don't be too predictable.

- Admire and inspire – ask questions about THEM.

- Make it fun and interesting. If you don't, someone else will.

- Pay attention. Eliminate distractions such as cell phone activities, the computer, and the television.

- Greet each other with enthusiastic and loving anticipation. (Golden Retriever style)

- Limit complaining – go with the flow. Flexibility is key.

- Laugh at each other's jokes – remember how to be charming and seductive.

KEEP YOUR RELATIONSHIP ON HIGH BEAMS! DON'T ALLOW IT TO DIM.

BE LOVING

♥ Support each other's dreams. Become each other's best friend and advocate. Have each other's back.

♥ Acknowledge and appreciate all that your partner does and let them know how grateful you are to have them in your life.

♥ Applaud your partner and the things that they do well. Brag about them in public.

♥ Treat your partner with the same care and courtesy that you would your best same-sex friend.

♥ Everyone wants to avoid pain and experience pleasure. Figure out what it is that makes your partner feel loved. A text, an email, a phone call, or a surprise visit can work wonders. No small gesture is ever small.

♥ Let your love grow and show. Fill your life with opportunities to express love and generosity. Caring for your in-laws, spending alone time with your partner's children, showing interest in shared charities are all ways to expand your love. Sensitivity is very sexy.

SPEND LEISURELY TIME TOGETHER – SHARE THE SAME RECREATIONAL ACTIVITIES

✿ Tennis

✿ Golf

✿ Skiing

✿ Bicycling

✿ Hiking

✿ Go to sporting events that you both enjoy.

✿ _____

✿ _____

✿ Go to concerts of your favorite musicians.

✿ Go to restaurants that you both favor.

✿ Enjoy some of the same television programs or movies.

✿ Cook together.

✿ Play cards, board or electronic games together.

✿ Fish, hunt, or do whatever it is that you both find interesting.

✿ _____

✿ _____

⚠ **WARNING:** This does not mean that you have to do everything together. Spending time recreating with each other is important. However, doing your own thing can be just as essential. Poker night with the boys or spa day with the girls is a refreshing endeavor and should be honored equally.

HAVE FUN WITH SEX

- Read erotic material together – books, magazines, etc.

- Watch erotic movies together.

- Go to stores specializing in sex paraphernalia and buy toys together.

- Read magazines like Cosmopolitan and Maxim that provide articles and tips for a healthy sex life.

- Go to a female or male strip club together if you both are comfortable with it.

- Go to Las Vegas (Disneyland for adults) together and explore.

- Experiment with each other.

⚠ **WARNING:** Our best sexual organ is the brain. Use it to stir things up and create a mood or urgency. Don't just grab and attack certain body parts. Foreplay is fun.

RECHARGE YOUR SEX LIFE!

SECURITY FEATURES THAT KEEP YOU MOVING IN THE RIGHT DIRECTION

There are certain fundamentals in a committed relationship that protect partners from experiencing unexpected breakdowns or serious crashes.

COMMUNICATION | LOVE & RESPECT | HUMOR | INTIMACY & SEX | FUN & RECREATION

SECURITY FEATURES

COMMUNICATION Communication is vital to any relationship. The problem is that most couples don't know how to communicate effectively.	
	Seek opportunities daily that promote communication. Commiserate over coffee, an evening walk, slip into a Jacuzzi, have a glass of wine before dinner or take a long, leisurely drive.
	Ask open-ended questions or statements that require more than a simple yes or no answer. Example: You seem distant tonight, what is that about? You said that you had a bad day, tell me what happened.
	Give your partner your undivided attention, noting both verbal and nonverbal communication. Listen with no distractions and make good eye contact.
	Pause and think before you speak. Write key points down if it helps. Be deliberate and not reactionary. Be concise and get to the point quickly.
	When communicating feelings, use "I" statements because you cannot speak for your partner. Never assume that you know what your partner is feeling or thinking unless they tell you.
	Try to empathize with your partner. Put yourself in their shoes and try to look through their lens. Attempt to see things from their point of view (POV), which may be vastly different from yours.

COMMUNICATION

If your partner expresses a different opinion than you about someone or something, don't attack them for it. They are entitled to their thoughts and feelings and it is unrealistic to expect them to share all of your beliefs.

Do not make global generalizations about what your partner tells you. If she comments that you spoil the children it doesn't mean that she thinks you are a bad father. You may want to follow up with a discussion about discipline options. If he says that you need to work out more, it doesn't mean that he hates your body. You may want to follow up with a conversation about fitness. Stick to the subject at hand and avoid becoming defensive.

⚠ **WARNING:** Men and women typically have different communication styles. Men tend to be more direct and succinct. As a whole, they are more linear and logical thinkers. Women tend to be more expressive and sensitive. They are often more emotional, becoming increasingly animated, visually upset, or tearful.

⚠ **WARNING:** Your partner is not a mind reader. You need to learn to communicate properly or run the risk of being misunderstood.

SECURITY FEATURES

LOVE AND RESPECT Without love, she reacts without respect. Without respect, he reacts without love. This creates a crazy cycle that couples get caught up in. (Dr. Emerson Eggerichs)	

	Do more to build your partner's ego rather than tear them down… even in jest.
	Focus on your partner's strengths not idiosyncrasies. Accept and minimize their flaws. Laugh off their shortcomings.
	Think loving thoughts about your partner every day and this will translate into loving actions. What we believe we conceive.
	Compliments go a long way. "You look amazing…". "I am so impressed with…" Let your partner know the ways in which you appreciate them.
	Boast about their special qualities and accomplishments to others in front of them. Go public with your adoration.
	Ask for your partner's opinion. This conveys that what they think is important and that you respect their judgment.
	Avoid correcting each other. This expresses disrespect for what the other person is saying.
	Neglect is the ultimate way to disrespect someone. Putting other people and things before your partner is the surest way to lose them. This includes your children. Don't ignore your mate while obsessing over the kids and their activities. We basically rent our children for a period of time and then they leave us to live their own lives. What's left are the two original people in the relationship.

⚠ **WARNING:** Respect yourself and the value that you bring to the relationship. If you don't love and respect yourself, no one else will either.

🚫 Do not try to build yourself up by putting down your partner. Not only is that disrespectful, but it has a way of backfiring.

HUMOR Lighten up! Stop treating everything like it is the end of the world. It's not.	
	Laugh often – about everything. Humor can be used to lighten a mood, to console, to redirect or diffuse, and to calm. (Nervous laughter)
	See the funny side of things. Think of life like a sitcom.
	Most importantly, develop the ability to laugh at yourself. Self-deprecating humor can be cute and sexy. Don't take life too seriously.
	Don't lose touch with the craziness in you. We all still have some kid within us.
	People want to be around people who are amusing and make life fun.
	A happy person equals a happy partner – seek out humor whenever possible, at movies, in books, and at comedy clubs.
	Humor heals and creates a natural high. Use it often.

⚠ **WARNING:** Be mindful not to make fun of your partner when they are feeling insecure or "less than." Laugh *with* them not *at* them.

SECURITY FEATURES

INTIMACY AND SEX Never underestimate the power of touch!	
	Touching your partner on the arm, shoulder, back, or leg in public conveys a connection. The same is true when holding hands, cuddling, or sharing a hug to be close. Caressing your partner unexpectedly, touching their hair or the back of their neck for no particular reason demonstrates love.
	Intimacy and sex are essential to any relationship. Sex, or lack thereof, is a major reason why people disengage from their partner and ultimately leave the marriage.
	Without intimacy and sex, partners tend to cheat on each other. "To a man, a relationship without sex represents a relationship with no love, no affection, and no emotional connection." (Sherry Argov) The same can be said for many women.
	Our best sexual organ is the brain. Ways to spice up your sex life are included in this manual on page 26. Experiment!
	Practice first date behavior often. Provide undivided attention, sit close with an open posture, lean in, maintain good eye contact, and touch.
	Flirt forever. Go for coffee together, meet for happy hour, or help each other at the gym. Don't be afraid to show public displays of affection regularly. Everyone recognizes and appreciates couples who are in tune with each other. It is an enviable position and outsiders are drawn to it like a magnet.

⚠ **WARNING:** Studies have shown that women tend to think about sex on a daily basis where as men think about sex on an hourly basis.

⚠ **WARNING:** People have different thresholds on how often they desire sex. We need to recognize our own individual baseline as well as that of our partner.

FUN AND RECREATION Don't forget to be playful!	
	Show an interest in your partner's passion even if it is not yours. You don't have to pretend that you love it, just don't dismiss it. Try to find ways to enjoy it as well. Whether it is football or tennis, share in the fun. If that is not possible then work around it. Compromise.
	Take risks. Learn something new together. "It's never too late to pick up a guitar or a paintbrush." (David Culiner)
	Share and alternate the privilege of picking a vacation spot. One may want to hike in the great outdoors while the other wants to go to New York and see Broadway shows. Try what the other suggests and you may end up having fun in a way that you never expected.
	Doing similar things that you did when you were first dating can reignite fond memories and old feelings.
	Double dating can remind you of what drew you together in the first place. Observing other relationships can be enlightening… good and bad. Either you will appreciate that you and your partner are still better than most or realize that you need to work on some things. Healthy comparisons can prove to be useful.
	Surround yourself with positive couples, those that enjoy being in a relationship. There is nothing worse than being in the company of the "Bickersons" or couple who fight constantly and create drama. The same can be said for your single friends who set out to prove that commitment is boring. Both sets of friends can negatively influence your relationship.

SHARING THE ROAD

FILMS, FOOD, MUSIC, AND FAMILIAR PLACES CAN TAKE YOU BACK TO A TIME IN YOUR LIFE

Name a comedy that made you laugh together as a couple.

Him:_____

Her:_____

What movie made you cry together?

Him:_____

Her:_____

What film did you both recommended to friends?

Him:_____

Her:_____

Name a favorite television program that you both scheduled to watch together.

Him:_____

Her:_____

What celebrity most resembled your partner when you first met?

Him:_____

Her:_____

What was the name of a favorite restaurant that you both frequented when you first fell in love?

Him:_____

Her:_____

Name a favorite appetizer that you love to share with each other.

Him:_____

Her:_____

What meal did you first prepare together for guests?

Him:_____

Her:_____

Name the favorite comfort food that both of you share on a regular basis.

Him:_____

Her:_____

SHARING THE ROAD

Name the song that you both identified as your special "couple song."

Him:_____

Her:_____

What was the first concert that you attended together?

Him:_____

Her:_____

Name a favorite artist that you both loved to listen to back in the day.

Him:_____

Her:_____

What was your favorite song to slow dance to when you first met?

Him:_____

Her:_____

Where did you share your first kiss?

Him:_____

Her:_____

Name the location of your favorite vacation together.

Him:_____

Her:_____

Recall a favorite memory of the first residence you shared together.

Him:_____

Her:_____

Where did you both talk about vacationing but have yet to go?

Him:_____

Her:_____

In one or two sentences, write your own epitaph.

Him:_____

_____

Her:_____

_____

What one word best describes you?

Him:_____

Her:_____

MAINTENANCE: THE WARRANTY IS UP — WHAT NOW?

BE AVAILABLE

Check with your partner throughout the day, even if it's merely a text to let them know that you are thinking about them. Share some office gossip or inquire what they would like to do for dinner. Show your loved one you are never too busy for them.

BE AWARE

Pay attention to warning and control gauges before a breakdown happens. Verbal and nonverbal cues are obvious if you remain alert and watch for them. (Refer to page 53 of this manual for a list of warning and control gauges.)

BE INTERESTED

Every evening take time to discuss how their day went. Don't focus solely on the children or retreat to your room. Display genuine curiosity and attention toward your partner.

BE PRESENT

If you notice that your partner is out of sorts, "How can I help?" is always a good way to get the discussion started. It conveys sincere concern and a willingness to be there for them. Even though you may not be able to fix their problem, offering to help is sometimes all that is needed.

CHECK-UP

BOTH OF YOU NEED TO DO THIS

On a scale of 1-10, how happy are you with our relationship?

Him:_____

Her:_____

What would you change?

Him:_____

Her:_____

What wouldn't you change?

Him:_____

Her:_____

What do you complain about me most with your best friend?

Him:_____

Her:_____

Name the thing that you love most about our life together.

Him:_____

Her:_____

Finish the sentence, "I would be happier if …"

Him:_____

Her:_____

Finish the sentence, "I want to be better at …"

Him:_____

Her:_____

Finish the sentence, "I will help you with …"

Him:_____

Her:_____

What do you hope that you will have achieved physically in the next five years?

Him:_____

Her:_____

What do you hope that you will have achieved emotionally in the next five years?

Him:_____

Her:_____

CHECK-UP

What do you hope we will have achieved financially in five years?

Him:_____

Her:_____

Where do you see us in five years?

Him:_____

Her:_____

Where do you see us in ten years?

Him:_____

Her:_____

Where do you see us retiring?

Him:_____

Her:_____

What do you see us doing in our retirement?

Him:_____

Her:_____

FILL THE TANK.

FUEL IS NECESSARY FOR ANY VEHICLE TO OPERATE PROPERLY. A SMOOTH RUNNING RELATIONSHIP IS FUELED BY THE FOLLOWING:

⚠ **WARNING:** Women have been known to tune into relationships better than men. That helps explain why 75% of women initiate the divorce. They have been dissatisfied with it and have been analyzing the issues for a longer period of time than the man.

⛽ Random acts of kindness can help energize a relationship. Taking her car to get it washed or taking his shoes to get them repaired are non-selfish acts.

⛽ Be receptive to each other's wants and needs. Keep your antennae up. Remain sensitive to your partner's moods and try to understand what they are experiencing. If someone is having a difficult time at work or if the children have been a drain all day, be empathetic to your partner's situation. You two are in this together.

⛽ Clean and polish your relationship. Buff out the scratches and treat it like the gem it is. Demonstrate the care and pride of owning a classic. Treasure what you have. Express your appreciation through words and actions. Pull out a chair for her or open her car door. Kiss him hello or pack a note in his briefcase thanking him for all that he does.

⛽ Change things up. Routine has its own reward but don't be habitual to the point of being boring. Just as your tires need to be rotated to maintain the proper balance and prevent blow outs, take note of the daily wear and tear in your relationship. Surprises don't have to be huge... they just need to be unexpected.

- Put as much effort into your relationship as you would your career, golf game, or anything else you wish to succeed at in life. Go after it with all your heart.

- Repair things as they start to break down. Don't wait until one issue causes a string of problems that become too difficult and costly to fix.

- Things change and relationships evolve. What you wanted when you were twenty typically changes when you are forty. Monitor the direction of your relationship and your life. Is the destination still the same as it was in the beginning and are you both on course to get there? Have you or your partner changed direction or lost sight of the original destination?

◎ Own your own stuff. Identify, acknowledge, and work hard to improve your individual shortcomings. None of us are perfect. We would do well to correct our own imperfections with as much fervor as we do our partner's.

◎ Don't project your bad mood or feelings on your partner. This is hard to do considering we tend to take it out on the ones we love. Try not to punish them for being in a better place. Rise up to their level instead of bringing them down to yours.

◎ Ask for what you need. Don't assume that your partner knows.

◎ Be positive. Approach life with a glass half-full attitude. How we think creates our feelings and our moods. Our thoughts affect our frame of mind and outlook.

◎ Reframe the negative things that happen to you in a constructive way. Did it send you in another direction... a better one? Did you learn a valuable lesson? What good came from the bad?

◎ Don't make mountains out of molehills. Stop fighting over silly things because life is too short.

◎ Develop the ability to let things go. Grudges are ugly and reliving past mistakes keeps you in a negative spiral. Forgive and forget.

◎ Tolerate your partner's flaws. Be kind toward their deficiencies and hopefully this will set an example for your partner to do the same.

◎ Anticipating potential problems and possible pitfalls before they arise may help to minimize the effects. This includes everything from recurring events such as PMS or monthly bill paying, to life-altering events such as unemployment or retirement. A major life change or life stage can be managed when acknowledged.

⚠ **WARNING:** Compassion is the key here. We are all flawed. Allowing for mistakes and understanding the human condition helps us be able to forgive. Blame and shame are counterproductive, fostering resentment and stonewalling.

TROUBLE-SHOOTING

VERBAL AND NONVERBAL CUES tell the real story. They are often indicators when something is not operating properly or when something may be very wrong.

- Going silent. No texts or phone calls
- Giving the cold shoulder, indifference.
- "Nothing's wrong."
- Pouting, playing the victim
- Avoidance at home
- Slamming doors... using heavy hands
- Unprovoked snapping (barking) at the other person

CHANGES IN ENERGY can signal that something problematic is happening.

- Loss of interest
- Diminished sexual response
- General fatigue
- Increased lethargy
- A decline in personal appearance

RAPID MOOD SWINGS may point to the fact that there is an unresolved issue that needs to be addressed.

- Quick to temper or to tears
- Inability to focus or concentrate
- Increased agitation and being edgy
- Becoming overly sensitive and defensive
- Becoming negative and bitter

NOTABLE CHANGES IN DAILY HABITS

- Increased desire to be alone
- Changes in appetite
- Changes in interests; i.e., suddenly listening to country music
- Frequently changing passwords on electronic devices or bank accounts
- Increased secrecy or decreased sharing

Even if things are running smoothly in other parts of the relationship, don't fail to address any area of concern however insignificant you may feel it is at the time. Your engine may be running effortlessly but if your tires are flat, you won't be going anywhere.

Major corrosives in any relationship are defensiveness and stubbornness. These will slowly eat away at all parts of the engine that drives the relationship.

⚠ **WARNING:** Don't ignore the warning signs in hopes that they will go away. They will reappear at the most inconvenient times. Investigating a problem early on can prevent costly repairs in the future.

"The Way to Your Car's Heart is Through Your Toolbox" – Deanna Sclar

BRAKE SYSTEM USAGE – Know when to put the brakes on during a conversation. Stop a disagreement from escalating. Retreat and retry at a later time.

TIMING LIGHT – Timing is everything. When approaching your partner with a difficult discussion or serious matter, adjust the timing for optimal results.

TUNING FORK – Remain tuned into your partner. Not just what they say, but more importantly, how they behave. Don't assume that they are okay because you are doing well. They may be experiencing a very dissimilar reality.

PRESSURE GAUGES – Internal and external pressures cause people to react to situations differently. Be cognizant of the various stresses and forces that impact your partner and influence your relationship. You may help them de-stress or release their tensions in a positive way. Then again, you may be able to take some of their burden on to lighten the load.

TORQUE WRENCH – Utilize whatever tools that will tighten the connection between the two of you. Subtle vibrations can loosen the fittings when going the distance. Do what is necessary to refasten them. Remember when you would stop at nothing in the beginning to get close to your partner? Recall what you did and do it again to renew the bond.

TOOLBOX

OIL DIPSTICK – Oil reduces the friction. Keep the love juices replenished for a closer and more intimate relationship. New romance full of infatuation and physical desire leads to sex. As the relationship matures, sex may begin by going through the motions if one party isn't in the mood and end with mutual fulfillment. It has been shown that by being present and willing, sensual yearnings get stirred up and reignited for increased affection. However, if this is repeatedly attempted and unsuccessful, a hormone or health-related issue may be at the root of the problem.

JUMPER CABLES – Recharging you or your partner's battery may require effort. It may be as simple as a nutritious meal, a good night's sleep, or a much needed vacation. None of us have endless supplies of energy. Jump starting is necessary when depletion of energy is apparent.

Deanna Sclar suggests having the proper tools on hand that help troubleshoot leaks, squeals, smells and strange sensations. What it comes down to is being able to recognize the signs of trouble and being sensitive to the signals. The tools in your toolbox will help with both diagnosis and treatment of the problems.

�֍ Admit when you know that you are wrong. Humility goes a long way.

✖ Be humble. Lay on the sword from time to time. Would you rather be right or happy?

✖ Self-effacing humor can be used to save the day. I am such a jerk, an idiot, a witch... clueless, blind, stupid, etc. Every one of us has felt that way before and admitting it shows strength not weakness.

✖ Offering to cook a nice dinner for the two of you so that you can talk demonstrates that you take the problem seriously and want to work it out.

✖ Flowers and cards may help, though they must be followed up with an acknowledgement of the dispute and an admission of your culpability in it.

✖ Buying your partner something that they have wanted for sometime will establish that you have been listening, that you care about their desires, and that you are putting forth the effort to make it right. This alone won't eliminate the problem. However, it sets the stage for some good dialogue.

> ⚠ **WARNING:** The apology must be honest and sincere for it to be effective. Sustained eye contact, a heartfelt hug, and unexpected tears convey genuine remorse.

THE DO'S AND DON'TS THAT PROTECT YOUR RELATIONSHIP FROM CRASHING AND BURNING

DO	DON'T
✔	✘

DO

1. Address the specific behavior causing concern, not the character flaws of your partner.

2. Stick to the subject at hand, leaving other issues and arguments out of it.

3. Remember to stick to "I" statements. "You" is accusatory. "I" owns it.

4. Listen without becoming defensive.

5. Give up the need to be right. Substitute it with the need to understand. Choose peace over justice.

6. Choose the right time and place to talk without distractions.

7. Be very selective with your words. Understand the power of your words and be deliberate, not reactionary.

DON'T

1. Avoid speaking in absolutes… "You always… or you never…"

2. No name calling

3. Do not give ultimatums. They rarely ever work.

4. No interrupting. If you need to interject a thought, ask permission to do so or write it down to discuss when it is your turn to speak.

5. Do not attack your partner because they have a different opinion than you do about something. Healthy debating can create growth for you both, but insisting that they must share all of your beliefs is narrow-minded and counterproductive. Agree to disagree.

6. Avoid arguing about everything. Don't sweat the small stuff and learn to let certain things go. Pick your battles wisely.

✔️ DO	❌ DON'T
8 Try to see the issues as challenging puzzles to sort out. They are opportunities for growth.	**7** Do not stonewall or refuse to discuss matters with your partner.
9 Negotiate compromises for a better outcome. The truth usually lies somewhere in-between.	**8** Do not hold onto anger.
10 Try a little tenderness. Empathy is incredibly sexy.	**9** Avoid dismissing your partner's concerns even though you may find them trivial.
11 Go the extra mile even when you feel stalled out. Give, give and give. Don't wait for the other person to do it first.	**10** No double standards. Do as I say and not as I do only works for children – occasionally.
12 Show appreciation, even for the things that are expected. Acknowledge effort.	**11** Avoid drama – don't exaggerate.
13 Apologize. Say "I'm sorry." Sometimes that is all that's needed.	**12** When you make a statement, don't negate it with a "But". That one word changes everything that you just said before it.
14 Forgive and forget.	**13** Holding your partner to a higher standard than you do yourself is wrong. High expectations only disappoint.
	14 Don't be too hard on your partner's family and friends. Chances are yours are not perfect.

🚫 Do not pick at the old wounds of your partner to prove a point. You may win the battle but you lose the war. Using their vulnerabilities against them is contraindicated. Violating their trust after they previously disclosed deep and painful secrets may irreparably damage your bond.

Calendars will help you deal in facts as opposed to perceptions. When discussing the frequency at which something occurs, marking them on the calendar tracks facts. This pertains to anything from the frequency of arguments, to sex, to workouts, to meal preparation or cleaning the house. Whenever the discussion contains "always" or "never", or when there is a disagreement regarding specific behaviors, a calendar will document their occurrence with greater accuracy. It may reveal patterns that went undetected, such as arguments taking place after visits with the in-laws or after parties where too many cocktails were consumed.

Sunday	Monday	Tuesday	Wednesday	Thursday	Friday	Saturday

CALENDAR

Sunday	Monday	Tuesday	Wednesday	Thursday	Friday	Saturday

Sunday	Monday	Tuesday	Wednesday	Thursday	Friday	Saturday

CALENDAR

Sunday	Monday	Tuesday	Wednesday	Thursday	Friday	Saturday

☎ Additional books and audiotapes located in libraries as well as the self-help section of bookstores are a good first step.

☎ Recording television programs that address relationship issues and provide solutions may be helpful. Including those that interject humor or comedy.

☎ Workshops for couples are available targeting everything from perspective taking to rekindling the romance.

☎ Magazine articles and periodicals often include useful information regarding relationships.

☎ Sometimes couples require the aid from a trained professional counselor. This person provides an unbiased opinion and acts as a third party to help guide the couple in the right direction. Couples learn valuable strategies that make for a less volatile and more manageable relationship. Whether the problem is more acute, such as a death in the family, or more chronic as with constant conflict, a counselor can help.

☎ Other professionals who may be of assistance include psychiatrists, primary care physicians, psychologists, ministers, priests, and rabbis.

☎ Classes in anger management, stress management, time management, conflict resolution, substance abuse, and addiction are available in most communities and may need to be utilized before the relationship will improve.

⚠ **WARNING:** Statistics show that couples wait an average of six years before seeking professional help for a failing marriage. By then it is often too late. Relationships are dynamic, never staying the same. If they are not moving forward then they are falling behind.

1. Chapman, Gary D. **"The Five Love Languages: The Secret to Love That Lasts."** Northfield Publishing, 2009.

2. Eggerichs, Emerson. **"Cracking the Communication Code. The Secret to Speaking Your Mate's Language."** Integrity publishers, Thomas Nelson, 2007.

3. Goldsmith, Barton. **"Emotional Fitness for Couples: 10 Minutes a Day to a Better Relationship."** New Harbinger Publications, 2005.

4. Gottman, John Ph. D. and Nan Silver. **"The Seven Principles for Making Marriage Work: A Practical Guide From the Country's Foremost Relationship Expert."** Harmony, 2015.

5. Hendrix, Harville. **"Getting the Love You Want: A Guide for Couples."** Henry Holt & Co., 2007.

6. Lerner, Harriet. **"Marriage Rules: A Manual For the Married and the Coupled Up."** Gotham, 2012.

7. McGraw, Phillip. **"Relationship Rescue: A Seven-Step Strategy for Reconnecting with Your Partner."** Hyperion, 2007.

8. McKay, Matthew, and Patrick Fanning, and Kim Paleg. **"Couple Skills: Making Your Relationship Work."** New Harbinger Publications, 2006.

9. Pransky, George S. **"The Relationship Handbook."** Pransky and Associates, 2001.

10. Richo, David. **"How to Be an Adult in Relationships: The Five Keys to Mindful Loving."** Shambhala Publications, 2002.

VEHICLE CARE

WORK AS A TEAM

THE FIVE FUNDAMENTALS OF PROMOTING YOUR PARTNERSHIP:

♛ **PRAISE YOUR PARTNER'S EFFORTS.**

♛ **SUPPORT YOUR PARTNER'S DREAMS AND ASPIRATIONS.**

♛ **COLLABORATE WITH YOUR PARTNER FOR DESIRED OUTCOMES.**

♛ **ENCOURAGE YOUR PARTNER TO GROW AND DEVELOP.**

♛ **BELIEVE IN YOUR PARTNER AND THEIR PROGRESS IN LIFE.**

ACCESSORIES

+ Children
+ Pets
+ Extended Family
+ Individual Friends
+ Couple Friends
+ Associates
+ Houses
+ Toys – boats, cars, campers, country club memberships

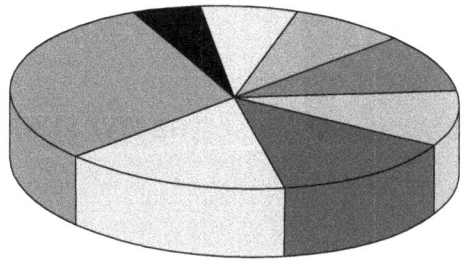

WARNING: All of these things impact your relationship positively and negatively depending on the circumstances. Situational and variable, they are constantly changing for the better or for the worse. They can be a drain on the relationship or a joy that you both share. All distract from the partnership to some degree. Accessories have the potential to bring you closer together or tear you apart.

(Circle the most appropriate answer)

Want children		Don't want children
Biological children	Surrogate	Adopted children
Natural birth / Midwife		Hospital
Let them cry themselves to sleep		Pick them up and rock them
Pacifier	Thumb	No Pacifier or Thumb
Cloth diapers		Disposables
Bassinet	Sleep in bed with parents	Crib
Breast		Bottle
Daycare	Nanny	Stay-at-home parenting
Spank	Time-out	Discuss
Correct		Coddle
Eat family meal		Eat what they like
Family dines together		Children eat first
Public school	Private school	Home-schooled

CHILDREN

Single child	Two children	Three or more children

Spouse first		Children first

Both parents work		One parent stays home

Athletics	Academics	Arts

Fast food okay		Natural food only

Buy them a new car	Buy them a used car	They help with auto expenses

Community college	University	Real-world education

Time frame on children: Now? Three years? Five years? Eight years?_____

What three qualities will make you a good parent? And those of your partner?_____

_____

What three characteristics of yours will make parenting a challenge? And those of your partner?_____

_____

+ Evolve to keep up with newer models. Be willing to learn different things and don't get stuck in a rut. Take classes together and inspire each other.

+ Strive to remain healthy in body and mind. Be the best that you can be and encourage your partner to do the same. Advocate for each other to preserve mental acuity as well as physical strength and agility. You are as young as you feel.

+ Do for others. Nothing feels better than being generous of heart and spirit. Work together for a better world.

+ With so many possibilities today to change a poor body image and optimize your potential, there is no excuse for "letting yourself go". We can all stand some improvement. Take pride in your appearance. Whether it be body contouring, hair restoration, or wrinkle reduction, it is completely acceptable to restore parts of you that cause you angst. Just don't overdo it.

+ You and your relationship are invaluable. Good memories and connections can never be replaced. Do what is necessary to understand, maintain, and restore what you have.

+ There is always the option of turning it in for a newer model, but all vehicles require a lot of time and effort to perform optimally. You may be simply exchanging one set of problems for another. Unless it is irreparable or totaled, there is always a chance to salvage the remaining parts.

CONCLUSION

Long-term relationships are not created by accident. Statistics show that fifty percent of all marriages in the U.S. crash and burn, resulting in divorce. Roles are constantly changing for men and women both inside and outside of the relationship. Stay-at-home dads have doubled in American households since the 80's. Women are now the major income earners in thirty-eight percent of U.S. households today. Single households are on the rise. The legalization of gay marriage is a major civil rights issue for politicians today. Another concern is the strain being created on our social security system due to people living longer. Society is changing and relationships need to evolve with the shift.

"Forever after" is a much sought after concept; however, it is in no way guaranteed. Though couples enter into marriage with the intent to stay together, the reality is that if they don't work at it, it won't work. Two for the Road is a simplified guide (manual) designed for men but applicable to all. The intent of the book is to get the conversation started. It breaks down relationship dynamics into manageable parts. Anticipating what lies ahead, being aware of the possible pitfalls, staying mindful and alert to what is happening, maintaining what is good and fixing what isn't allows for increased success in committed relationships.

THOUGHTS

THOUGHTS

THOUGHTS

INDEX

INDEX

Thank you, **ROB IANNI**, for believing in me as a person and as a writer. You possessed the confidence to demonstrate that men do care as deeply about relationships as women, they just go about it differently.

Thank you, **LAUREN SEEFELD**, my daughter, who traveled with me for many years on my journey. I hope with all of my heart that you go bravely on your own excursions and that they take you places you never thought possible.

Many thanks to **ALL OF MY GIRLFRIENDS** in Michigan, Florida, Minnesota, California, Nevada, and Texas, who begged me to write a relationship book that men would actually read. To these frustrated women who left the men they loved or were left by them, as well as to those who successfully rode out the storm, this manual is for you. The raw conversations that took place around the kitchen table inspired this book and validated the information in it.

Thank you, **DAVID** and **LORRAINE STANTON**, my parents, who remained best friends through their long and not so perfect marriage. Though I wanted to live by their example and listen to their sage advice regarding relationships, it would require time and several failed attempts for me to grasp their wisdom.

Thank you, **DR. ROBERT BROWN**, former Chair of the Counseling program at Oakland University, who emphasized that relationships cannot be perfect because the people in them are not. Relationships, however, can be managed and ultimately enriched.

Lastly, thanks to **MY EXES**, most notably to **MARK SEEFELD**, my husband for over twenty years. I believe that we all did the best that we could do in the moment and that had we known better we would have done better

www.ingramcontent.com/pod-product-compliance
Lightning Source LLC
Chambersburg PA
CBHW080052280326
41934CB00014B/3297